ANATOMY OF LOVE

Gbanabom Hallowell

Sierra Leonean Writers Series

Anatomy of Love
Copyright © 2017 by Gbanabom Hallowell
All rights reserved.

ISBN: 9789988869731

Sierra Leonean Writers Series

CONTENTS

Foreword v
In Search of My Love 1
Sunset Between Us 3
Kissing Carefully 4
Every Flesh Has Had a Sore 6
Waiting in Vain 8
Daybreak in Loveland 9
A Metaphor for Love 10
Marriage of the Absolute 11
Love is a Big Bang Theory 12
Dear God, I am in Love 14
The Adam and Eve of Love 15
The Devil's Romance 17
His Father's Son 18
Love Among the Ruins 19
The Knife of the Kissing Tongue 21
Septik Putin, My Russian Love 23
The Year of the Love war 24
Love is No Apple in the Garden 25
Anatomy of Love 26
What is in a Name? 28
Drop 30
Wedding Bells 32
Wash My Skin Where Love Hurts 34
Eclipse of Love 36
Love Was Not Built in a Day 38
Accident and Love 39
Feeding on Love From Samuella's Eyes 40
Lovers, Beware of Monday 42

Planetary Woman   44
Letter to Khadi   45
Wine, Women and Writing   46
Ebony   47
Cold War   48
Approaching the Bench of Love   49
Pick Up the Phone   50
Ah, My Phone Rings   52
Call Me Through the Phone   54
Telephone Conversation   56
Phone Call   57
Let's Talk About Sex   59
Groan   60
Love in the Air   61
No Awards For the Bridegroom   62
Send Me Your Pillow   64
There Goes My Lover   65
Love in the Harmattan   66
Lethal Love   67
My Sierra Leonean Lover   68
Woman of My Clock   70
Stop Searching My Face For You   72
Broken Hearted   74
A Lady Waits in the Dark For Light   75
Not Ready To Tango   76
I am Waiting Under the Regional Tree   77
When Should New Dates Ask For Money   78
An Ode to a Brand New Kiss   79
Of Moaning and Groaning   80
Confession of an Aged Poet   81
I Love You Between Your Eyes   82

Born Aborted **85**
The Trial of an Aborted Child **86**
Lilacs of the Night sky **88**
Lilacs of the Night sky: The Hand of Magic **90**
Lilacs of the Night Sky: Shades of Blue **91**

Other Books by Gbanabom Hallowell

POEMS

Hills of Temper (1996)
Drumbeats of War (2004)
My Immigrant Blood (2006)
Manscape in the Sierra: New & Collected Poems 1991-2011(SLWS, 2012)
A Little After Dawn (2013)
When Sierra Leone Was a Woman (2014)
Don't Call Me Elvis and Other Poems (SLWS, 2016)
The Art of the Lonely Wanderer (SLWS, 2016)

EDITED BOOKS

Leoneanthology:
Contemporary Short Stories & Poems from Sierra Leone
(SLWS, 2016)
In the Belly of the Lion:
An Anthology of New Sierra Leonean Short Stories (SLWS, 2015)

FICTION

Gbomgbosoro: Two Short Stories (SLWS, 2012)
The Road to Kaibara (SLWS, 2016)

WAR DIARY

Tears of the Sweet Peninsula:
May 25, 1997 and the Sierra Leone Civil Conflict (2005)

FOREWORD

Anatomy of Love is the piping hot collection of poems by Gbanabom Hallowell, the doyen of Sierra Leonean poetry. To be sure, Hallowell needs no introduction. This is not his first volume of poetry. He has eight collections of poems in print, apart from other works that he has published.

It was at the Annie Walsh Memorial School where I had my Secondary School education that I first met with Gbanabom Hallowell, who had come to our school as a young and enthusiastic teacher. I lost touch with him after that, but reconnected with him about five years ago through a mutual friend, a couple of weeks before he launched one of his other volumes of poetry, *Manscape in the Sierra*. Over the years, I have found him to be a very passionate and committed writer, a lover of books and a true believer in mentoring or helping others, especially budding writers to move up the creative writing ladder.

Hallowell lives and breathes for poetry. Poetry has found a haven for itself in his heart and is lodged deep within his DNA. A compulsive poet, he has written poems on a wide range of issues. He bends every emotion, situation, experience and idea to his will and subdues them in poetic expression. His style is distinctive; his voice is still urgent, as in his previous poetry and the atmosphere of the poems in this volume almost takes us to the world of Blake's *Songs of Experience*.

Anatomy of Love is a compelling collection of poems that makes us look at the world anew–this is not unusual for Hallowell. The title of his work suggests that the poems in this volume will examine the nature of love and reveal how it works. In fact, as I remarked to one of my colleagues, I thought that in his *Anatomy*, he will serenade us with lyrics that focus on the beauty of the international emotion of love. On the contrary, Hallowell deflates our expectations by making room for a medley of issues, emotions and images in his collection that we can hardly categorise under the theme of love.

Some of his poems explore the relationship between men and women; man and God; man and motherland; father and child; and the individual and society. Others deal with love that is reciprocated; love that has turned sour; or love that is unwelcome. The interesting irony though, is that with Hallowell, some of the poems that promise to talk about love actually go down roads that lead to anything but love. And in some of his poems, as soon as he talks about love or kissing, he swiftly associates it with suffering, pain, hypocrisy, betrayal and violence.

The language, tone, and imagery of certain poems in this volume are not destined to reflect our conventional picture of love. Hallowell crushes our hopes and refuses to jettison his own view of love and of life. It is scarcely an accident that even in his love poetry, he ends up outside the green world of Illyria, waiting, searching, and ready to 'rip' our 'hypocrisy' from our 'oesophagus'.

Hallowell's searching intellect is never off duty. From the very first poem to the last, we are given an insight into the mind of a man who loves his lover, his country, his poetry and who is often painfully aware that love can be unrequited, inconstant and cruel.

Apart from a handful of tender poems, Hallowell's verse is muscular and his language has a hard edge to it. Through irony, metaphor, repetition, personification and paradox, he often achieves a contrast between the tone and imagery of his poems in such a way that though he attempts to talk about love, he ends up speaking the 'brutal language of love.' As he asserts in 'A Metaphor For Love:'

> The spoons walk up to me
> To eat my heart while the kitchen
> Knife aims for my soft flesh…

Throughout this volume, the images, of the cemetery, death, disease, gorged eyes, knives, blood, crown of thorns, ripped oesophagus and the black mamba, to name a few, are startling, especially because we find them in unexpected places.

The poems in this collection are highly commended, not only because it will give us joy to read the works of someone who has contributed to carving a place for himself and our motherland on the world's literary landscape, but also because they open our eyes to new ways of seeing and interpreting the universe.

We should also read Hallowell's *Anatomy* to dream. Or rather, we read his poems and dream that perhaps one day we too can rise to the height of his accomplishment.

Elizabeth L. A. Kamara
Head, English Unit, Department of Language Studies
Fourah Bay College,
University of Sierra Leone

April 2017

Anatomy of Love

IN SEARCH OF MY LOVE

I long for the color of your love.
The water inside of me is a breath of this longing.
Thinking about you, my spasm is taking a bite
On the skin that made love
To your skin when it was dark,
While the room fed on that darkness,
Sinking a lion-tooth in your flesh.

I am coming against your new century
In one day to love you like a lion,
To touch you where your flesh
Is a pound fresh on my bone.
Give me some salt water where I am thirsty
To drink down the beast of the moment.

I am your black Mamba
Coiling where my nerve is awake.
I secure myself around my being
Connected to the tremors
Of the river. I am a poet when you
Stand in my heart, when you walk up to my mind
In a blue dress, loving me across the face of forgetfulness.

Inside this red bandana
I am full of you; take me to the Alps
Now that we have conquered the height
Of the Everest and love me against
The breasts of time.
Pull me against your warmth

Like a cup of hot water that runs over
The liquid of love in this ebb and tide.

I am up against myself, searching
For your eyes inside your looks,
For your skin inside your flesh,
For your breath inside your beauty,
For your thirst inside your hunger,
For your sweetness inside your taste,
And for myself inside yourself!

SUNSET BETWEEN US

In the aftermath of it all
The golden ring rolled
Back to me without a wind.
The veil tore into two
And scattered its white
Powder on the floor
Between our tired legs.

A sudden Venetian
Night dropped its dark
Mood on our Christian
Wedding, verse after verse.
An allegorical divorce
Slipped away from
The choir finding its way
Back to where a wedding
Had occurred a decade
Before it was to be a marriage.

We took back our first dance
Holding it from the first few
Strings of the base guitar
And ripped the vocalist's
Hypocrisy from between
His oesophagus, and
We stepped on it
In the cold slab of the floor.

KISSING CAREFULLY

Taking orders from himself,
The convert kissed his toe
Before putting it into his shoe.

The vagabond kissed
His anger before swallowing
It into his hollow heart.

The miner kissed his hands
Before digging into his pit
To search out his baggage.

The widower kissed the head of the corpse
Where the lips of the dead
Had moved up to, like a sky.

The preacher kissed
The bread to manifest his
Hunger in the time of farming.

The climber kissed
His exocrine on skin for
The sake of his endocrine.

The universal man
Kissed his days for the sake
Of his priestly order.

Anatomy of Love

The exile kissed his loneliness
For the universal shoulders
Of his immediate sunset.

The wanderer kissed his mantle
For the sake of the quiet taste
Of his silence and the journey thereafter.

Gbanabom Hallowell

EVERY FLESH HAS HAD A SORE

Sex is a shock when it hits hard,
Bringing down the yoke with a 9/11.
Sergeants of smoke pick up birds
With white plumages through fuzzy
Eyes and a New York of legs
Plays the trick, sweeping steps.

Every evening the world loses
A new lover to the spider's web
And to the predatory spider's embrace.

Such is it in war torn Allepo,
Now at a bloody mess.
So much was it in my Sierra Leone
When it too was raped by war.

The taste of blood is even
Sweeter in the time of peace
When every bird is chirping
The language of the beak.

Sex is urgent by day as well
As by night; by the stone of its
Own mind it brings the world
To its knees as the earth douses
In blazes of more and less screams.

Upon reflecting on this truth,
The mortal flesh is joyous

Anatomy of Love

Except in its own joy, moving
Itself through to the age of pain.
It may cover itself in black or
White, in riches or rags, yet
Every flesh has had a sore.

WAITING IN VAIN

The caustic wind came and was
Unable to open the book.
In the pages of the book
Spiders played tickly tricks.
The wind with all its caustic
Speed could not open the
Pages where love was trapped
In a lifeless world and seamlessly so.

Who is waiting for me by the graveyard,
To love me in the hour of death?
I moved three nights against
Three *darknesses* when they kept me
Waiting in vain after they hid my love
In their black gowns.
Whatsoever hour I have waited
I have not mastered the tricks
Played by the spiders in the season
Of the caustic wind
Unable to uncover
The wisdom buried in books.

I have waited one minute too
Long for the wisdom of the book
Of love where spiders are
Having fun with children of the
Dead and I am trapped
In the emptiness
Of a lifeless storm caustically.

DAYBREAK IN LOVELAND

Dawn wiped its mouth with
An invincible attitude and I was
Able to clearly see my long lost
Love walking the forgotten street

One Sunday morning
I retrieved a sight from the long
Book of love, after
Its journey from
The forest of night, carrying romance
In the heavy case of my chest

The city is obsessed with
Its own love affair and it is
In mid-knife crisis, and
All the green lovers
Are the sharp edges those
Knives are aiming at

Gbanabom Hallowell

A METAPHOR FOR LOVE

Under these circumstances
The door pleads with me to open up for love;
The window wants to peep through
Me for affection's sake; the road
Wants to walk all over me coyly.
The sun wants me to shine
In its face while the moon
Electrifies my body with beams.

The books read me
Philosophically to romance in pages.
The Lovejoy sits on me
In the living room watching me
Watch love's electrifying gait.
The spoons walk up to me
To eat my heart while the kitchen
Knife aims for my soft flesh
To understand the brutal
Language of love.

My pillows know more about love
Than I do—So they come to me
In subtle dreams. The covers
Play tricks with my body.
Tonight I am a bed to my bed,
Taking back all the pressures
Long sustained from my plough.
Tonight I confess my innocence
Under such circumstances.

MARRIAGE OF THE ABSOLUTE

The bride wears a hat that knocks
On the sky with a hammer.
The truth in her eyes is different
From the truth in the groom's eyes.

She has red eyes and the
Groom's eyes are undecidedly
Colorless. The fingers that wear
The rings are missing, so the
Toes are opting for the vows and
The goodness that come
With the caravan of noise.

A wedding of fresh doors welcomes,
Knocking down entrants with gloves
As white as grey and dresses made
In heaven with suits of future
Shrouds. The caravan passes by through
A Hymnal of voices singing
Tired biblical verses with organs
Made with funereal notes.

Day-dressed pages, with angelic
Smile cover the couple's death
Warrants with a drama till
The old Sun sheds its tears
In a twenty-four hour vigil.

LOVE IS A BIG BANG THEORY

I touch the palate of your love with a stick
Of mind and my soul longs for that baptismal kiss.
At once, I depart from myself to search for the man
I was in the vibrating flames of the candles
You lit the hour we first made love.

Now that my hour is missing in your twenty
Four hour day, I am existing as a miserable
Time in your quick eye.

I hate my days when the blistering hands
Of night wrap around them, and you are not here
With a new stick of candles.

Whatever took your eyes off me has set a nation
Of one man on fire, and in due course
I have become a lover on the fringes
Of extenuating circumstances, pleading
For my soul to be returned to me so that I can stand
As a jar at tables visited by hungry souls.

O that you may think about me in the alphabet of our
Primal point when the leaves suddenly sprout green
Under our wild valleys.

O that you may tend to that memorable silence the first
Time we kissed in our scatological approach to romance.

Anatomy of Love

If the end has come, let it not be at the finish
Line, where, like a cipher,
I can be erased by the hand that did
Not make me. Therefore, send me
Off with the kiss that first
Broke our innocence and saw my soul
Leaping out of place forever---that way I can
Live as a dream and return to the century that
Brought us together, and I will touch your still
Lips with the fresh fingers of an artist.

DEAR GOD, I AM IN LOVE

There goes my dead lover,
Oh God. She can't die dismiss-ally.
I live in a shade because of her
Grave that breathes dead air at
My vulnerable skin.

She should breathe alive again, dear God.
I would have died in her
Stead if it didn't mean not
Able to make love to her again
On her breasts, chest to chest.

There sits my love inside her corpse
Mourning her death in her
That came to her black nostrils.
Oh God, see how her fatal face
Cries with pain, running down to her legs.
Please bring her back to life with
Your divine breath---my love
Will be more grateful than Eve's.

O taste and see how my faith
Is strong oh Lord of my love.
Resurrect me in my desire
And my love in the radiance
Of your craft that toils in your sleepless
Fingers, O gifted hands!

THE ADAM AND EVE OF LOVE

The day is cruel on Monday.
An hour goes by severely
On a dog's brow,
Manifesting human
Love through dog bones.
Then a dirty fly sits on the lip
Of an alcoholic
Contemplating sex
In human thought, howling inside
It's tiny head for man to go forth.
Gargantuan man, walking in his
Own stead, makes love in his head
Many more times than in his
Bed. But the giraffe is not envious
Of man living like a king in his
Own creation; for from the green
Leaves of the tree the giraffe comes
Away with both the thought and
His cranial desire to make love.
At once, blood runs through
The man, observing
The agony of animal desire coming
Through the beast of no nation.
The king of the jungle,
After mutilating a dear,
And hacking its meat, throws it
To the sky, chases after
The queen of the jungle
To make love. In the

Gbanabom Hallowell

Instance of becoming
The humanimal, man goes
For the kill laid in his comfort,
And she is called woman!

THE DEVIL'S ROMANCE

A patch runs across the devil's
Dress where his blood of lust
Drops the drip of love through
Intravenous romance.

The devil is in three cards and
His deck is a soiled finger
Tempting the owl and the bat
To lick his bloody hands all night.

The devil loves with dark faces,
In dark phases, in places where
There's a shrill of yore. He drinks
To conquered souls with no spirits.

He is the preacher who turns left
In a world of only right;
The miner with his talisman
Under his pit while digging for more.

HIS FATHER'S SON

(for Ken Saro Wiwa, Jr.)

For the sadness of his happiness
Ken Saro Wiwa lived old to die
Young, looking after his father's
Voice in the land of the Blacks
Where shell lit all the oil they mined.

He died very young but lived long
To crown his father's head with
The thorns the crowd placed on
The tree of good and evil.

He was his father's son and he
Fathered his dad after they killed
Him on the nameless highway.

He goes now to tell his father
To accept his sad death which
The enemies had planned with
Flesh and bones.

LOVE AMONG THE RUINS

My love for her has had
An environmental setback.
The sun comes up in
The middle of the night to shake
Hands with dawn.

It is my romance that gets locked
Up in the time that stills.
The sea now wants to travel
The desert to warm up its
Waters of wine.

It is my embrace that gets wet
By the tributaries. The rain
Is rising for the kiss
Of the sky; often with
A storm around its
Climbing rope,
Thorns bruise me.

I'm a victim of an
Environmental gangrene.
My love is stuck in the mud
And the sky looks at me
With a low eye.

My love is waiting in
The midnight hour
For the madness

Gbanabom Hallowell

Of the world to pass by while
I sail in a boat, rowing
Around my sixth,
To save my love.

THE KNIFE OF THE KISSING TONGUE

There's a rascal rattler in the
Mouth that licks to taste
The world through other people's
Tongues via a metal of agony.

It lies in a lowly crawl to wait
Like the rugged cross. An orange mamba
Of smooth taste, bears the pain and
The tastes that sail through the mouth.

The orange mamba spits fire and
Kisses with a sting in an instant,
From hate to love.
It writhes in its own orbit and
Its cyber space of its fastidiousness.

Plenitude of spasm,
The rattler is swift, and with
Its pancreatic agony, that viper
That only recently loved one,
Tongue to tongue, has stung another, flesh to flesh.

A mouth of ample hate,
Capable of love, all with
A single heartless knife that
Slaughtered the Christ, Socrates,
And Julius Caesar, also slaughtered
Romeo and Juliet.

The rattling tongue
Is attracted to the rose as well
As to the cashew against both
Sentimental and draconian backdrops.

SEPTIK PUTIN, MY RUSSIAN LOVE

Of doggerel vacuum, amputated
Rhymes, Septik Putin, my love
Is constipated with overtime
Affection while obsessed
With me.

I am contaminated with his
Russian affection that
I could inhale a million
Miles away.

When we meet we collect around
The strong sense that
Separates us. We love
Each other in silence.

Love is at its zenith when it leads
To its suffocating net where human
Breath has to be forced
From the food pipe.

Septik Putin, my love is crunchy,
Expressing himself in hollow places.
For that matter our love lasts
Longer in public spaces even
If it's humid in private places.

THE YEAR OF THE LOVE WAR

Seismic shifts, nuclear bombs,
Intercontinental romance, ballistic
Embrace, sustained arsenals
And endemic contests with ferocious
Weapons conquered hearts laid
For the game against the life
Of opponents--settled scores
For love and for the hand
Of the rose in a bundle
Tied with a heart.
Flowers with gunshot
Wounds, dark smoke of mortal
Love rose above to the helpless
Distance of the sky in utter temper.
Global warming instigated by
Deluded affection and fatal
Attractions ended infatuations
In white bathtubs and death
In blue dresses taken over by
Red blood scorpions.
Lovekill came in serpentine dates
Blazing in ungodly night hours,
In search of the igniters of their
Torches and then went into action,
Slaughtering rivals with Damoclean
Swords and with the hatred
Of the brutes, they impose love.

LOVE IS NO APPLE IN THE GARDEN

His branding came as a digesting
Organ, looking at the soul he talked to about love,
About singing her the portal
Sailing of boats, about the
Centimeter length of affection,
About the nocturnal patience
Of pleasure; this feisty element
Carried the transgression
Of the brute soul that carried
A heartless man educated only
In the libido of his own attention, and making
His kangaroo case in the guise of love,
He plunged into her soul catastrophically.

O chaste O serene sentiment
Of her soul that opted against
The rough shod, and a void
To wait for the late eve sun
Plodding behind the protective
Hills; elemental lass, coming down
The road with a bob, or with
A brown comb stalked in her hair
And teeth whiter than themselves;
Gazes no farther than the playground,
Chatting on the teacher's assignment
And rummaging her mother's dream
Of the Babel to fly to, the airplane
To board, to reach the living waters.

Gbanabom Hallowell

ANATOMY OF LOVE

To manifest love one needs
A stupendous thought wrought
From the temple of a single stone.
And with a sedimentary desire
One goes to the clear mind of
A small river and kisses it with one's
Lips three times in a trinity of
Oath blessed by an imaginary
Dove with white feathers ready
For the kill, sacrificially speaking.

After the offering of oath is burnt,
One must turn around in one
Desperate moment and sprint back to town,
Speaking the tongue of sex in
Supplication, knowing that
One would be loved in return.
In the event that one is not loved
In return, one must shave one's
Head with a crude knife until one
Feels the blood of the skull dripping
Through one's skin like a noiseless
Rain, and one could then utter
The name of the girl in one's mind
Until the girl could be seen loving
Herself in a sizeable mirror.

If that fails, one must conjure
The spirit of the god of love,

Anatomy of Love

Make him look abysmal in a feminine
Sense until he can stand tall,
Man to man with a gender accord.
In that moment, one must be
Brave enough to look Medusa
In the eye while ripping the heart
Of a god and swallowing it alive.
If one is not turned into a stone
One is sure to be turned into
A lover in the hand of one's desire!

WHAT'S IN A NAME?

At the beach
I met a man who ate
His name
And then stood erect
Like a verb.

Adjectivally speaking,
He turned his oblong
Head at me adverbially.
"Stop looking at the waistline
Of my lady," he said.

I interrogated him regarding where
He though my eyes were.

He said, "I owe the preposition
"That brings this woman
"To the plate of my heart."

I reminded him that he was
No longer a human after he had
Swallowed his own name.

He looked at me in frustration
And said, "Oh, I'm finished.
"Could you kindly loan me
"Your name, I certainly need
"A name for her to call me by."

Anatomy of Love

I agreed because I knew that
After that moment I could collect
My name from between the breasts
Of the woman I met at Lumley Beach.

Gbanabom Hallowell

DROP

I made love
To her
In the time of war

And I saw
Stars roaming
My head
And the stars
Got bigger
And
She lost
Breath
And I breathed
Snort and
Snorted
And we
Pressed
The gas
The gas
And I got
Suffocated
I got
Su
Ff
Oc
At
Ed

And I

Anatomy of Love

Oh dear
It

Ra
In
Ed

Hiro
Shima

WEDDING BELLS

In the event that our love hits
The bottom doxology let us not
Invite the priest to offer us
An atonement. The birds will fly
Above us with envelopes of letters
Bearing invitations to the place
Where the march was made.

A new perimeter is approaching
The riverbank of our love and
Already my heart is sinking within.
I long for the verses that took
Our hands and put them together.
One wonders what wind is seeking
To put these hands asunder?

I am becoming an acre in the
Desert seeking oases of love
From your breasts, which once
Saddled me along the burning
Grains of sand. To say I have
Forgotten those wild stories
Is to say I never loved in the eye.

Shall we stand under the night
When the moon passes by to
Visit the back mountains?
Shall we ask the mother in the
Moon's face to renew our vows?

Anatomy of Love

To milk us with the leftover
Of the young gods who got
Wedded yesterday?

WASH MY SKIN WHERE LOVE HURTS

A swift width has expressed
The extent to which I have always
Confessed my love for you.
Against every chance to keep
My head safe above waters
Of the Loveland, I have held myself
Ostentatiously high like an evening
Patio where lovers retire to begin
Again, and to call human questions
By their answers, and by the scores
Of the love of one being to another
Spasmodically chasm.

My ocean is gathering me unto
Itself in its most sacred reserve
To wash my skin where love hurts
When it embraces my humanity
With insufficiency and with
A naked palm.
I have known sleepless
Moments travelling from afar
To tease me with a cold left hand.

Agony is lying beside me and
With me because love is denying
Me the moment of its time.
At once I leave my own presence
And seek after the elusive wind
With an elusive mind.

Anatomy of Love

A testimony of mosquitoes visit
Me tonight to speak to my black
Skin whose tenderness has gone
With the wind of yesterday.
Tonight I am religiously faithless
And for once, my window
Is heartbroken faithlessly.

ECLIPSE OF LOVE

A little flint came running across
The face of my thought
In beats of Deuteronomy,
With an eyelid of ember,
In seven directions,
Speaking of rivers
Of serenity and of love, and
Of the absence of lovers
Who should become birds
On the electrical anniversary
Of all of Africa's forgotten gods
Of love, and their escapades
On the branches of green trees
Along the drainage of the river.

Seismic manuscripts of drums
Of love, their heroes and their
Prowess, come alive in songs
Of tired lips but leaping hearts
Of dry bones of lovers who come
To the bonfires of memories
To warm the eyes of the youth
And to build their romance in
Their black skins before
The eclipse of love.

Tonight there will be
The eclipse of love up above
The egos of lovers with a flint

Anatomy of Love

Of diamonds burning in the moon,
In the palm of the Sun god;
Tonight the fires from between
Our palms shall illuminate
In small withdrawal of spaces,
And in that eclipse, I shall find
The lioness in my soul.

Gbanabom Hallowell

LOVE WAS NOT BUILT IN A DAY

The giant muscles of love were not
Built in a day. The erected pillars
Of romance took a century
Courtship to soar the vast expanse.

The first kiss lingered on the eyelids
With a shy serenity and calm bravery
Until after the retaining walls
Of confidence stood as tall as
A historical Cotton Tree
In the middle of itself.

Bringing the wind to a halt,
And pausing the flow
Of the river, the Roman jaw surged;
And with the courage of Pushkin,
Took an African advancement
To meet the flower, lip to lip.

The nails of commitment should
Bring the joints together, connecting
Cements and boards, zinc and
Corner stones, wires and rails,
Balusters and arms,
To ensure a smooth embrace.

ACCIDENT AND LOVE

After the accident
I picked up myself in the mouth
Of her love.

This morning when I was escaping
Death, a coin dropped in the bottom
Of her heart where I had invested
A caring hand.

If I cheated today it was against
Death for love. Two hands worked
On me with the mind of evening
And I took the evening that came
From her eyes with a ring of roses.

Several men can die in a single
Man yet only one heart can search
For love even in the peninsula
Of pain where odd objects always
Lock in the dark.

Tonight I am reinvented because
I come to the same love with
A mind in a technical embrace
Believing that I am the lover and
And the pool of love.

FEEDING ON LOVE FROM SAMUELLA'S EYES

"...take a break from those dark poems," Samuella Conteh

My heart was pagan dark love
Flashing only to strike
The death knell in devildom.

The bitter teeth of dark gowns
Followed me as a metaphor
Stroke after stroke, and a good
Poetess, Samuella had learned
To go by her fear each time
She encountered me verse after
Verse, with half her mind behind
Her back. I approached her with
A stick with which I drew
A line against her sand until
I got her to love me sadistically.

In this hour of her unconditional
Love for me, Samuella has
Killed me after my gruesome
Name. The dark man in me
Is in Samuella's bloody hand,
Dead in his choke. A white sheet
Is over me and I now smell
Of roses, red crimson roses!

Tonight Samuella loves me
In new lyrics. She comes to me

In comfortable images and my
Head is up against the bright
Sky where there are no accidents!

Gbanabom Hallowell

LOVERS, BEWARE OF MONDAY

Considering that I had an accident
On Monday, what else shall stand
Between me and the leftover
Of the week? What is sacred about
The iron that takes one to one's
Lover and plots one's death after
A good sex?

Why is Monday suicidal
In the morning and yet offers
Dream breasts in the evening?
Is it possible to die on a day that
Conspires against itself?
What ultimate window exists
In the sadness of Monday, being
That the day offers itself
To death and to life?
How many more tricks can
Monday keep in its belly of darkness
That an older Sunday cannot decipher?

The Monday I was supposed
To die was utterly aggressive,
Even going ahead of Tuesday
In a grey suit. What technical
Doubts flushed its face one may
Never know, but Monday
Is the only tenant in the mansion of the week,
Looking so readily broken

Anatomy of Love

In wit and in thought.
On any fine morning it can come as
A badly disappointed lover, dressed
In a good suit but broken buttons
And an unkempt collar; so even on
A good morning, Monday can
Be a nasty day to make love
In the dark with a familiar lover.

PLANETARY WOMAN

In light of the accident that left
A scar in my heart, I salute you,
Woman of substance; come forward
And walk ahead of me romantically.
Appeal to my vertical sense, now
That the gold of love burns across
My heart with a vested right hand,
Reaching across to the left
To achieve an embrace.
Hospitalize me in your bosom
And feed me your love intravenously
With the love in your soul.
I have an eye laid on your horizontal
Beauty and across that stretch
I long to go down on my knees
And be equal to your moon, star
To star in the eclipse of your galaxy.
Planetary woman, take me into
Your solar system with
The lightning of your tongue
Approximately through your ninety
Degrees affection distributed
Across the elements of your body.

LETTER TO KHADI

Dear Khadi,

I tried calling you last night but the moon came right into my mouth from the sky and tonight I am worried that the silver bird will not take us to the clouds.

What fire will burn tonight from our celestial hearts I do not know; and I'm aware you do not want to long for the distance of Saturn.

And tonight after the moon, I sit here in the rain, drinking wine unable to write a love poem for the absence that took you from our dining table.

Sheriff, a friend of mine will deliver my heart to yours when he arrives London tonight.

WINE, WOMEN & WRITING

So to offer myself to them I wait
For inspiration through the tender
Whisper of my three looks
To the triplet in a single glass.
My profound trinity speaks to
The sea, rising from the igneous
Rock and I hold a glass of wine,
Women and the writing roaming
My head. A dragon wraps itself
Around the muscles of the rays
Of the sun, and in one breath smells
The powder of wine, women and
Writing and takes a stare at the
Blue stature of love affectionately.
My three aces have evolved into
A single soul, feeding on the waters
Running through my indefatigable
Spine, in all appropriate measures!

EBONY

You stand lucrative in the window
Of my heart, and I am calm, waiting
For your oil on my black skin,
For your whisper in my ear
And for your hand in my hand.

I contemplate your body in verse,
Its graphic elevation against my
Animal tide, the ebb and flow
Of my eyes behind their glasses.

A sudden road passes me by
With its urgent shiver and at once
I surrender to your image after
The body of smoke that invaded
You in its brief history of time.

I whisper your name against your
Moon and the backdrop left in
Your wake of emergence in honor
Of my warm human existence.

Let us move toward the shadow
Of our desire and cloth ourselves
Body to body until we hear
The morning train screeching
On the savannah rails of our Egypt.

COLD WAR

Temperature
Minus a degree of affection--
Rivers of the heart freezing.
The dawn of winter is on
Our bodies without thawing.

Night of dark punctured
The gradual moon,
And the day blinded in our
Eyes, pissing the pus
Of the punctured star
Of our love at first sight.

Fierce knives flipped
From the soft skins
That once knew each other
In soft punches in the ring.
The nails of the rain fell
From their packets
Of clouds, grey and steel.

It became a cold war
In the heart and
In the conscience,
In the bosom and
In the quick breath;
In the heath where
The wreath lied waiting.

APPROACHING THE BENCH OF LOVE

At an opening ceremony
Where my heart was already
Closed she benched me
Under the sun profusely.

The flower was cold from
Being dropped from
The palm and being that
Summer was too slow
On its journey, love was to
Approach the bench.

In the space of time that
The sun came with
A solitude of anger and
Rested its irons on my
Chemicals, the truth
Germinated raw about love
And the loss of life involved.

The sorrowing heart and
The parting soul make
A claim to death between
Their twists, and the blood
That runs from the mortal
Flesh cares a hoot
For the dying ember of love!

Gbanabom Hallowell

PICK UP THE PHONE

Faggots egged me from death
And I saw a missed gall under
Which lied a repeated death
For my Lazarus. I must touch
Her soul before the end of this
Brief span of second chance!

Pick up your phone, I am journeying
Through the nozzle of the wind
To swim in your ear. Pick up, pick.
The dial is beating in your heart
And you know it's my number
Singing in your soul. You know
It from beneath your memory.

I am the black boy beneath your
Morning breath calling you on
Your phone like thunder calling
Rain to pelt the earth.
Fall for me my rain, my storm.

The clouds are dark and I am waiting
For you in my phone.
Pick up and touch me where the
flesh is weak and where my heart
Pauses until the rain wets me.
Pick up, pick, my number
Is counting against its ringing.

Anatomy of Love

Don't send my voice to the machine
To leave my blood tasteless.
Taste me now in raw blood
And water. My salt is tired.
Pick up, pick, my line is cracking.

Gbanabom Hallowell

AH, MY PHONE RINGS

Who calls below the belt of love?
Who bleeds memory in my heart,
Sending figures to rattle the snake
Beside my bed? I am up against
The hour, jumping unto your ringing
Tone, palpitating seconds after
Seconds. Stop calling me!!!

What violence enters my phone,
Leaping with hysterical madness,
Crowing in the black night, long
And deep against the solitude
Guarding my four walls. Stop calling me!!!

The life of my phone is up against
Itself, and now its fingers aim
For my ears, approaching like
A toll and ringing as if to dead
Coffins, breathing dead and gore,
With the persistence of hell,
Wringing deep. Stop calling me!!!

Who calls the troubled gods into
My home through the innocence
Of my phone? Ah, who calls,
Who calls when my hands refuse
To pick your ear besides my toes?
Who stays alive to wake herself
From death through my fear?

Adieu! Adieu! Stop calling me!!!

Persistent caller, now, deep red
Blood runs up the throat of my
Phone, and its voice is cracking
Up like a blasted rock, and my
Phone is weak but courageous;
And I tell again, stop calling me!!!

CALL ME THROUGH THE PHONE

I rise from the hourless glass,
A receiver in my ear whispering
Hunger in urgent
Tenses, waiting for your call.

Call me by my airless name
To sail it through the electrical
Handset, to touch my lobes softly
And tenderly like wings of air.

Call me in the midnight of my
Life and not a little later when
The birds come to take their feathers
Back from my bare body.

Call me at the promise of the
Rain, when the trees ruffle
To make green love in the open;
When the desert masturbates
In the bottom of its oases.

Instead of missing your call
Let me miss a heartbeat;
Instead of missing your call
Let me miss the oracular
Exchange between earth and
Space and the extended galaxy.

Anatomy of Love

Call me through the phone
To cover the light years between
Us as long as it is to assure me
That the love I placed in your
Heart has merged with your psyche!

Gbanabom Hallowell

TELEPHONE CONVERSATION

In a single breath of salutation,
I surrender my body and soul
To you existentially.

Your body comes against mine
As smooth as soap with quick
Friction. It sounds more ecstatic
On the phone in your single breath.

Pull over in your limousine assisted
By the wetness of your tongue.
How you roll it now in your handset
Clicking the breath without perfume.

You visited Victoria's Secret:
I feel that initial gait toward
That secret in your pauses to
Touch the hot pants in the unpacked
Bag, crispy--inside are a colorful
Restless hotties ready for your
Skin and the skin now in voice
In this telephone conversation.

PHONE CALL

In the rain waiting for your phone
Call to clear the twilight from
The handkerchief in the clouds hanging
High like a ceremonial
Bandana to wipe the waiting in my eyes
Where the black is
Blue and color is meaningless.

I am waiting for your phone call.
Call me where the sky is clear.
Call me because I am dying and
Living in the empty space of time.
Call me on your phone
Before the grey clouds move over
My head and bring their anger across.

Call me on your capital phone.
Call me beside the accessories
In your fingers, playing the waiting
Game while I wait for that call,
That damn call eating my soul away.
Call me before I grow old
With lazy pants twisting my middle.
Call me on your phone so that
I can smell your sweet voice.

The leaves of time are coming
Against me, pant after pant and
You have still not dialed

My future wrapped around your lipstick
Fingers, playing the red buttons
Of the strange piano in the patio.
Somebody tell her to call me on the phone!!
My world is in the
Dial where her fingers are avoiding
The crustacean crow.

I am dying for a single phone
Call from her made in her heart.
I am under the weather waiting
For the ray to ring a call from
Her phone until I can stand among the bulrushes
Where I have always taken my phone
To answer the past voices saved in my head.
Call me please, on your phone—
I am waiting in death!
Call my fucking dead soul!

LET'S TALK ABOUT SEX

About its noisy silence
On daily faces plying
The earth for all the wrong
Reasons, buried in all the
Wrong places with the right
Coverings and lying
On broken beds because
The bed frames refuse
To take the bodies in
Unless they come in pairs.

About the blind moments
Felt in taste and dying
On tongues in pink patterns
And wrapping like a cloud,
Spreading their legs across
The wide expanse of orgies
With one viral sting.
Bodies die on each
Other's chest and
Resurrect in one groan
Panting over the sky to rain
On us all who wait for it.

GROAN

It begins with a tiny voice
Squeezing through the
Larynx with a vibrating
Calmness, deafening the
Ear from within its without.

It sends an organ of breath
Through the keys of a piano,
Making all its notes rumble
And the sound engage
In an accident across waves.

It pours the nose in its two
Nostrils with a solid pang
And draws the cat's life
From the human breath
Unless of course death is asleep.

LOVE IN THE AIR

Reach for the air and pick up
A white handkerchief from among
The pillars of the sky. Wipe my
Face with the love on your mind
Reserved for me in your virgin
Forest. Love me with your left
Breast and warm me with your
Right breast. I look up above my
Head and I behold you in the free
Sky among the long legs of the
Flowers where butterflies mate.

I am below the ladder looking
You up among the birds of the
Air and you smile to me from
The towers of our love.
You drop my love heart after heart
And I receive it experientially.

I long to spread my love on the
Back of your smile, visiting Saturn
And Mars where your legs have
Already stretched nearer to
The fireside made for lovers
Of the lilacs hanging in there.
The sky, like a silver of blue oceans,
Breathes calm waters of love
Into our hungry lungs.

Gbanabom Hallowell

NO AWARDS FOR THE BRIDEGROOM

The publisher is up against
My back, a love affair scandalous
To my throat and to my eyes,
Keeping the bridal dress between
The pen and the book dutifully
Choking the daily life in me.

I am in love with the color that
Separates my eyes from my
View when your vision journeys
Through between the sights that
Connect us, the distance that runs between us.

To what category of awardees
Should my identification
Be displayed if the publisher
Should look upon my sweat
With pity, knowing that
I offered my throat to the knife
Of his dream without a Bachelor's
Eve, or ate the Apple before
The manuscript was sent to him.

Today I love the life of a manuscript,
The characters who fall in love
In them within the mind
Of the writer who dares to sit on the writing desk
With a taste of vinegar on his
Lips and a rude mind in his hands.

Anatomy of Love

Today I have my eyes set toward
The Gold Coast where my publisher
Sits in his professorial order
With fifty copies of my eighth
Collection of poems wishing
To fly to Freetown to romance
With my eyes, my heart and my
Soul before it gets its things
To leave and to wander!

SEND ME YOUR PILLOW

Its dark over here, pitch black,
And yet I cannot sleep for lack
Of the net of night in my eyes.
Send me your somber pillow lying
Below your lower thighs, looking
Directly up where your breasts
Tease the whispers of my night.

I am lonely tonight, waiting
For a miracle, also known as
A pleasant surprise, that approaches
The believer on a wagon of gold.
I am waiting patiently like a tired
Penny ready for a pound of
Promotion to fetch more of you.

You loom large in the dark
In a wet form with less than an
Ample hour compared with the
Urge eating me within. You drop
Into a phantom with a quick candle
In your lazy night leaving me as
Empty as the widow of romance.

Send me your pillow, the soft
Side of your pillow that screws
Your ear lobes with a virginal
Taste against a fierce body of
A lizard preying on top of a rock.

THERE GOES MY LOVER

She goes away by her body taking
Away that authentic gait that
Always sweeps my heart away.

She stands under the moon
Implacably becoming
The milk of the moon
And the moon becoming her.

She wades the water of the stream
Combing her hair against the
Tide and swimming toward her
Shadow in blue hopes.

When she is in love she goes
Against the burning ray of the
Sun to reach me with a warm
Embrace drawn from under her
Armpit and the courage of her
Soul, the belt of her strength.

LOVE IN THE HARMATTAN

Tonight my desire is urgent yet
I remain man enough to break
A conversation over partnership:

To stab myself a dozen times
On the chest that covers the heart
With a flesh that could lose the
Trust reposed in the breasts.

To open up over my own sea and
Rush against the flow approaching
With the bellows of ebb and tide.
To stand on the brink of a river
Murdering a Pharaoh in one sink.

To be gentle within my human
Chromosome with a pink safety
To appeal to the establishment.

Tonight I gather myself under
The whisper of a wind flowing
With love and a hopeful lover.

LETHAL LOVE

A sheathe, a fierce shard of light,
Shards of eyes blinding vision.
A Viking history of love under
The yoke of wild imagination
In mad houses, in utter taste
Of instant salty blood, in shards
Of pain, joyous pain and drain.

Orgies and the smell of Brazilian
Hair and the fever of thirst hold
Fashion concurrently in broken
Hearts soaked in rain in booze
Alcoholically demanding dead
Silence of breath in shards of
Gas and Gas Chambers.

Lighthouse of groans of fire burning
The soul of couples in shards,
Blinking hope and death in a single
Lust within the skylark, painting
It's own artistry, leveling the bunker
Where sex is the subject of its
Own woes in the guts of mortals!

Gbanabom Hallowell

MY SIERRA LEONEAN LOVER

You stand above sand dunes,
Above the clouds on your feet,
Tall, with a vertical sense of paradise.
You gather yourself among warm
Waters with a notion of the country.
You love the countryside with
An urban sense and with the trust
Of the corridors the country strides
Among its senses of history.

Woman of the Sierra show your
Lioness above the waters of the
Hour and reach for your hills among
The mountains! I love your
Queen-dom jingoistic-ally
And I seek for the hand
Of your heart in my soul.
Live in me because you are
A country and beside me,
Live romantically, O Sierra!

Technically you are my country
But you are a solid woman too.
In your dual being you are the
Sense of my pride and I live in
Your single double-ness as a crowded
Lover, loving myself in a dual sense.
You spread yourself among
The waters of the Scarcies in

Anatomy of Love

Touch with all the waters of your
Name in body and in soul.

Tonight, in this full moon, up above
Among the lilacs of the night
Sky, I surrender to your beauty
Aesthetically, and I return to your
Embrace with a metrical mind
Not found in the most musical
Poem ever written below you!

Gbanabom Hallowell

WOMAN OF MY CLOCK

The hour I have
Waited all day long
Died at night in the clock

And still you have
Not walked through
That door to my heart

Too many dead moments
Keep resurrecting in me
And now my cemetery
Stands in its solitude

And suddenly
Your shadow walks
Through a common

Door landing in wings
And walking toward me
It rose in a black dress

Woman, your shadow
Stands before me empty
Black and boneless
Even bloodless

Now I hang on
The stiff hour of the clock
Hoping that I can

Anatomy of Love

Turn back the hands
Of time on us both

But I am waiting
For the ticking machine
Tick tock tick tock
Tick tock tick tock
Tick tick tick tock

STOP SEARCHING MY FACE FOR YOU

My face is ebony.
Black oil drips from my nose
And you watch the contours
Ridging beside the eyelid underneath
The calmness of the lashes.
Stop searching my face for you!
Stop looking blandly into my eyes
Because your eyes pierce me
Through the heart, and I am left
With tears running down my face.
Stop looking into my eyes with
The electrical flint in your eyes!
You seduce me with the fire in
Your eyes and the eyes in your
Face and the face that looks
Into my face. Stop searching
My face for you! Stop your
Ebony from meeting with my ebony!

BROKEN HEARTED

My woman has gone
On flight in the hay.
The husk rice flew with her
By her diligent shoes
After a gentleman passed by
Our door speaking in tongues.
My woman is gone bare chest-ed,
Naked to her middle with little
Left below her waist.
She went away in the Harmattan
Leaving a cold wind to chew
My lips even when the sun stood
Still to warm the cold earth.
My woman of long years
Went away in the dark in the nude.
She took her heart with her
In her hands and left all her clothes
In the bedroom close to the rumpled
Sheet and the bed we had
Not touched together in months!
My woman has gone in a single
Breath with a long sigh.

Gbanabom Hallowell

A LADY WAITS IN THE DARK FOR LIGHT

There is a blue girl in the dark
Waiting for the light to spill so
She can gather herself around her beauty.
A heart is pounding in the dark
Room for a light to glow so that
The owner can show the world
What value lies in the dark room.
A tentative room is silent in its
Oblivion, doors unlocked, expecting
A white light to claim a blue lady
Waiting in the middle of her darkness.
The lights come on plural legs
Swinging like a candle in the wind
To show on the mortal face
Of the most beautiful lady who
Ever walked the earth in her day!

NOT READY TO TANGO

I ran back into myself
Because I sensed someone looking
Into my eyes longer than anyone
Ever did. She stood still for a while
Before she knocked into my heart
Wishing I had really seen myself
In her eyes, trying to find me home.
All the while I stood beside myself
Watching her making conversation
With me sprawled in the realm.
She held a gold ring toward me
Wishing I could stretch my fingers
Toward hers. She held a tear back
And talked about children as being gifts
From God. She said she saw
A vision of a house beside a sea
And I stood at the front door waiting
For her to return with a bouquet
Of flowers and a smiling face.
I took a step backward and held
A breath in my heart. I gathered
Away from myself and shook
My head in the sad wind, and
I withdrew my fingers from the
Open, and I turned around and
Walked toward the rough sea
Where the crowd continued to
Dance to music from a single
Guitar in some busy fingers.

Gbanabom Hallowell

I AM WAITING UNDER THE REGIONAL TREE

I am waiting under the regional tree
With my roots running on the surface
Of the earth and the earth running
In my veins like a sprinter chasing
After the gold in the eye of the distance.

I am waiting for your palm to soften
My own palm, to soften the skin of my
Heart as I feel the prick of standing
To wait for the hour when you shall come
To stand beside me, to stand beside me.

I am waiting for your wind to come as air,
To breathe beside my own breath
And to navigate around me with a spherical
Mind and the mind of a distant star
Burning bright with the eye of your love.

I am waiting for your silence to come in a roar,
To burst like a wind and drench my desert
So that even as I wait, I wait with a patience
Under the regional tree with my roots
Running on the surface of the earth.

WHEN SHOULD NEW DATES ASK FOR MONEY

When the date is old
And I have drunk
My soup and beers too,
When her tongue
Loosens to show a vein,
When the teeth remain
White and befriend
Her bloody tongue
On a daily basis,
When the clothes she
Wears keep their perfumes,
When the dollar
Rises below her eyes
And when the banks
And all their ATMs
Are on strike.

AN ODE TO A BRAND NEW KISS

Drunk in my virtual being,
I have been kissed
With the lips of blade
And my two worlds
Of life and death
Breathe impatiently
To own this mortal lips.

Let the night that built
Me perish in the day,
For no time shall furl
Around this romantic
Coat of mine. The sea
Is black, mirroring my skin.

My teeth went to sleep
Shedding their steel.
I will celebrate on
The campus of Yamba
And wait for another
Day a new Celia will
Rise from the dust!

OF MOANING AND GROANING

And then your adrenaline
Conquered my brain.
It was already falling off
February 14 and nobody
Was dead in the beleaguered
House, but I moaned the flesh
The woman groaned through
The dutiful nose.

The wind twisted
And fell on the dark bodies.
Two souls perished
Under the weight
Of the bodies of night.
The power of the pipe liquid
Was in the throat of a dry dam.

It rained and the wretched
Souls suffered a heart attack
Through the lavender buds.
New modes of moaning
Told themselves in cries
And a victim was heard baying.

Tonight I have drunk
Like Adam seeking
To know why I am
Without a dress of leaves
And why Eve is no

Longer Eve and why my
Brother Farouk does not look
So well in the beer bar any more than does Mallam!

Anatomy of Love

CONFESSION OF AN AGED POET

My left eye gorged in love
The bottle of hope
Broke on my un-eleventh
Hour and a godless rain
Fell on my only flour.
I baked my love instead,
I cried over my loafless love.

My right eye gorged.
I felt the window
Of love rattling in the wind
After my brothers had
Harvested their pies.

I am here waiting for that
Female poet who forgot
To love me in her prime!

Gbanabom Hallowell

I LOVE YOU BETWEEN YOUR EYES

in the end, my love,
the day shall walk
Away, with its bright
eyes sticking in mud
and in the blistering
night and I shall love you
between your naked eyes.

fascist thinkers, let
me into your theory,
for I am full of love,
and of the full pint
of oil. Siddhartha, tease
me with your left
because my right hand
cannot hold a flower.

i am the finger clue
coming against deserts,
against stagnant Niles
smelling of orchids
and of the life of dead
things raging in their own
Sea. I stand beside

myself, half a thought,
looking like a god, no
longer able to stop

Anatomy of Love

---

the world from showing
love while killing every breath.

fuck to that sweet rose,
that tired muscles
of the wretched sea
and the darkness of the
careless mountain.

fuck to my bread,
close to the plate,
the little finger kissing
itself in the lips, the knife
lying on the table
after cutting its own
bread into two halves.

fuck to my pain mixing
with unpardonable tears,
wetting my face each
time a love drinks
the hemlock.

speaking of which,
fuck to Pushkin for
loving too much
with the taste of flower
in his rabid mouth
and a worthless sword
below his other belt.

Gbanabom Hallowell

just before I say fuck
to you, I must rip off your
blatant eyes for ease
of the literary pain
you are condemned to.

so fuck to you!

BORN ABORTED

You killed the flesh
Poured my blood
But I came forth

You gnashed your
Teeth crushing me
Between your fingers
And yet I came forth

You panted in hate
Murdering me in
Cold blood against
My hurting you
And yet I came forth

You ripped me apart
Because you were raped
A crime I didn't commit
And still I came forth

I came dead yet I came
My name is not rape
My soul is tabula rasa
Mama, I am not guilty

You deprived me of a name.

THE TRIAL OF AN ABORTED CHILD

Night-mid creatures
Pause in foetus
Dame of earth
Crawl and not talk
Pink death
Sad sorrow steam
Spoilt of the earth
Apple tree people
Naked foetus
All mankind
Born or aborted
Knife world
Kingdom divided
Blood doctors
Doctored blood
Flesh of dust
Killing cry
Dust to dust
Mama weeps
Tenured criminals
Bring forth
Chameleon babies
Umbilical abscesses
Man hurts woman
Baby built on
Life support
The image of (wo)man
God aborted
Bruised apples

Anatomy of Love

Falling bruised.
Earth wind fire
Sorrow people
Killing census
Bathing money-child
Weep weep weep.

LILACS OF THE NIGHT SKY

Sad lover
Besides his little honey stick
As each roller drops besides its romantic fire
Views the sky in lilacs of thirst,
Beholding a land above land, environmentally
Looking brisk in a timeless clock
Against the patience of a loving
Mind without arms of wings to dare
The sky of lilacs where magic
Is taking over the brink of the stars
Bringing out of it the solid water of waiting.
A mind was already thawed
In the oasis a block of liquid laid
Here below the sky brought about by two searching eyes
Looking for the lilacs of a princess in a white dress.
The hour continues to cough into oblivion
And still the lover remains sad,
Sad in the face of the stars growing into moons of love.
The wind is slowly hushing into the dark earth
Lighter and lighter like a sad white feather in flight.
The sad lover sits still beside his little stick.
Up above the sky the night is waving a hand
And the twilight is rocking the pillars
Built with the sobriety of the love sprinkled
Like stars, burning hot and cold and winking
Across the quick expanse.
There is a cross going across my heart
And fire traverses the skylark of seasons
Holding the suspense in the eye.

Anatomy of Love

I love the ladies wandering up above,
Wandering on the brink of the stick.
Little hands on the savage temper of the
South wind, the east wind, the north wind and the west!

Gbanabom Hallowell

LILACS OF THE NIGHT SKY: THE HAND OF MAGIC

Magic is in the air
And in two thoughts.
A living handkerchief
Is lurking in the sky
Beside two clouds
Of birds, aiming,
With a destiny
In their beaks
For the twilight
Of the sky where lilacs
Are ambling.
The lost lover
Is wandering the night sky
With eyes that could soar
Above birds

LILACS OF THE NIGHT SKY: SHADES OF BLUE

I am in the Shade

I am in the shade
Of a tree because
A man is standing
On my left toe.
I am bathing in sand
Because the sea
Is on strike;
Yesterday I went out
Without my heart,
Searching for a vacant
Woman;
I laughed to the miner
Who had drunk
His tongue down
His own pit.
The face of two
Did not save his tears,
So I decided to cry
With him, even
Shedding a sweat
Where he dried up
Quickly.
After all my pursuits
For a woman and
My sadness for
The miner, I put
On a resolved face

Gbanabom Hallowell

To return him and wear
My heart to come
Out again.

I am Scared Tonight

I am sacred tonight.
The man bit my flesh
For a little truth of fun.
I am a miner, and
I have the hunger
Of greed. Working
For the driver whose
Train runs on my back.
A man is approaching
Me with gold
In his stomach.
I am the overseer
Who must tell
The boss that a fellow
Is in his fetish
Tonight that
Must be killed with
A knife.
Yet I have my own
Sorrow limping
In my stomach.
My friend told me
To digest it, but
I do not have
The intestine for that.

Tonight I feel the rain
Whispering in my
Stomach with a whole
World turning
Into its own planet.
Give me free!

Ever Since

Ever since
I was informed
That any poem sent
Here will be published,
I have learned to climb
Forest trees,
To eat my apples
In the dark,
To settle for simple
Music,
To cater for my own
Sentiments,
To live like a broken
Plate with water trickling below
It's temperature.
I am particularly
Lost in my little fear
That the whisper
I am familiar with
No longer can
Maintain a secret.
There is a thread

Leading to my being
Put out of this forum
No longer sounds
Like the poem
My father read to me
Before my birth.
I am moving waters
From the bottom
Of rivers after clearing
Them of their slavish
Warmth.
I stand corrected
If I have become
A quick judge
In the face
Of a drunken
Magistrate;
But I have to defend
Myself every drop
Of my blood!

www.ingramcontent.com/pod-product-compliance
Lightning Source LLC
Chambersburg PA
CBHW032145040426
42449CB00005B/406